Fish-ing
Derbyshire

Published by:
Arc Publishing and Print
166 Knowle Lane
Sheffield S11 9SJ

Produced By: Chris Keeling

G000240930

ISBN: 978-1-906722-18-0

ACKNOWLEDGEMENTS
I would like to thank the following for their
help in producing this guide:

Kevin Miles
Ed Heath
Sam Broomhead (Front Cover Photo)
All fishery owners and angling clubs who have kindly
provided information.

May 2011

Arc Publishing and Print
166 Knowle Lane
Sheffield
S11 9SJ

W E L C O M E

There is a wide variety of fishing opportunities in Derbyshire. More southerly the lower reaches of the River Derwent and the River Trent offer coarse fishermen great sport. The River Trent is gaining back its popularity with good catches to be had at Swarkestone. Aside from the rivers there are numerous gravel pits, ponds, lakes and reservoirs to try.
I have fished many of these Derbyshire venues from being a boy. Barlow Fisheries on the border with South Yorkshire is where I started course fishing and it is still as popular today with young novice anglers.

Like many other fisherman, my time on the bank is limited, but I like to grab a few hours fishing whenever and wherever I can. Always bearing this in mind, I have put together, my sixth book "Fish-it 6 Derbyshire".
I have included all the details you need to find the venues and hopefully give you an idea of what's on offer at each, before setting of on a lengthy (and now with petrol prices so high) expensive journey.

Fishing attracts so many people, perhaps it is the solitude in often beautiful surroundings. Of course there is also the eager anticipation of catching the big one! The bank side can be almost hypnotic and the desire to catch just one more fish has spoilt many a meal.

I hope you find this book useful and wish you good luck, good fishing and remember - "A bad day's fishing is still better than a good day's work!"

Chris Keeling

C O N T E N T S

3

A B O U T   T H I S   G U I D E

To help you locate a fishery, the venues have been arranged in alphabetical order and split into two sections.
Their approximate location has been indicated on a map on page 8

Green Section   Derbyshire Fisheries

Red Section   Derbyshire Rivers

Each page contains details of a fishery,
with information on the following:

Ticket Price: All day ticket costs plus details on OAPs, disabled and junior concessions.

Directions: Usually from the nearest city or town, or from the closest motorway junction.

Description: A brief outline of what the fishery looks like plus details on features such as islands, depths and the best places to fish.

Types of Fish: List of species present, many with estimated weights.

Rules/Bans: The restrictions set by the fishery on type of baits, hooks etc.

Number of Lakes: The number of waters available to fish at the venue.

Facilities: What is available at each location i.e. cafe.

Telephone: The number of either the owner, angling club secretary or match organiser.

Sat Nav: Post Codes for use on satellite navigation systems.

S P E C I E S / S Y M B O L S

Most commonly found in the Derbyshire area.

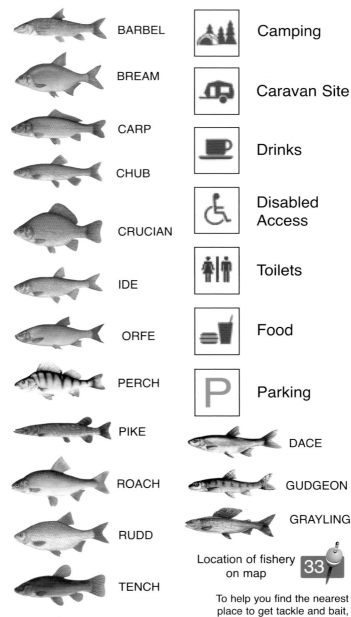

Fish	Symbol
BARBEL	Camping
BREAM	Caravan Site
CARP	Drinks
CHUB	Disabled Access
CRUCIAN	Toilets
IDE	Food
ORFE	Parking
PERCH	DACE
PIKE	GUDGEON
ROACH	GRAYLING
RUDD	Location of fishery on map
TENCH	
TROUT	

Location of fishery on map **33**

To help you find the nearest place to get tackle and bait, you will find a list of fishing tackle shops in the Derbyshire area on page 61

5

Blood Knot

This knot can be used to join two lines together, start by overlapping the ends of the two lines.

Thread the end of your line through the eye of your hook.

Twist one end round the other line four times and pass it between the two lines.

Do the same with the other end of line, making sure the previous step does not come undone.

Before pulling tight wet the knot to lubricate this also make it hold better. Trim off the two ends.

Pull on the loose end to tighten. Trim the line.

Half Blood Knot

Used mainly for joining hook to line.

Pass the free end underneath the line and bring it back over the line to form a loop

Continue to loop the free over the line about four times.

Pass the loose end between the eye of the hook and the first loop.

Pull the knot as tight as possible and trim of the end.

Double Overhand loop

This knot is used to create a loop at the end of a line. Also known as the surgeon's loop.

To begin, double the end of the line back against itself.

Tie an overhand knot in the doubled line.

The doubled end should then be tucked through the loop again.

Pull the lines tightly so that the loop makes a knot. Trim the two ends.

Water Knot

This knot can also be known as the surgeon's knot. It is useful for joining a lighter hook line to your mainline

Hold the ends of the two lines alongside each other so that they overlap by about six inches.

Take hold of the two lines and make a wide loop.

Holding the two lines together. Pass the ends of the line through the loop four times.

Pull the lines tightly so that the loop makes a knot. Trim the two ends.

POLE FISHING
FOR THE BEGINNER

Of all the different methods of fishing I've tried, I haven't found any of them as accurate or as easy as pole fishing. To be able to place your bait and feed to the exact spot, sometimes only inches from an island or group of reeds is what makes pole fishing so productive and fun.

TACKLE NEEDED

A Pole

Poles come in various sizes, from 4 metres (usually called a whip) to poles of 18.5 metres. They also vary dramatically in price as well, this is usually governed by weight and rigidity. The lighter and straighter (no droop at the end) the more expensive they are. I recommend a pole between 11 and 13 metres, stay away from the smaller telescopic ones. Many tackle shops have poles ready assembled for you to handle, make sure you are comfortable with its weight and it feels well balanced. Test that it takes apart smoothly. If possible, get a pole with a spare top section as they enable you to rig up for different species and size of fish.

Pole Rigs

Experienced anglers can make up their own pole rigs but beginners are advised to buy ready-made. There are plenty of quality ready made rigs available for as little as £2.99. These rigs come with a main line with a loop on the end (used to attach the line to the stonfo connector at the tip of your pole). A float sits below it to cock it nicely in the water and a length of lower breaking strain line, which has a spade end hook tied to it. The float and shot can slide down the line and be adjusted accordingly.

Pole Elastic

The elastic that runs through the top sections of your pole cushions the fight of a hooked fish and allows you to play it. Elastics are graded in sizes 1-20.
The following list is a good guide for the beginner:
1. For small roach and perch for example - use a No4 elastic with a 1lb hook length and a 2lb main line.
2. If fishing for small carp and tench or skimmer bream use a No8 or 10 elastic with a 3.5lb main line and 2.5lb hook length.
3. When fishing for carp up to 12lbs use a No16 to 18 elastic, and a main line of 8lb with a 6.5lb hook length.

START TO FISH

Fishing Position

Get your seatbox in position. Ideally, when sitting on the box, your thighs should be in a horizontal position, at right angles to your lower leg. Holding the pole correctly makes it comfortable for long periods and prevents backache. For a right handed person you need to rest the pole across your knees with your left hand supporting it. Put your right forearm along the end of the pole and firmly grip the pole with your right hand. Have close to hand - your bait, landing net, disgorger and anything else you may require for your days fishing. It is important to have your pole roller in the correct location. The pole has to be well balanced in your hands when it leaves the roller - this prevents rig tangles when shipping out.

Start Fishing

You have set up your pole and plumbed your depth - so now you are ready to fish. Make sure you have between 10" and 20" of line between the tip and float. In more windy conditions you may want to lengthen this. Feed your swim with groundbait (if allowed) plus a few bits of your hook bait. This is more accurately done using a pole cup which can be fixed to the end of your pole. Put your bait on the hook and ship out your pole trying to keep your rig in the water as this prevents tangles. Lay the rig on the water lengthways. The shot on the line will pull the line under the water and cock the float.
Enjoy your first pole fishing day!

Fishery Location Map

High Peak and Dales

New Mills

Buxton

Bakewell

Dronfield

Chesterfield

Staveley

Bolsover

Shirebrook

North East Derbyshire

Matlock

Clay Cross

Wirksworth

Alfreton

Ripley

Amber Valley

Ashbourne

Belper

Heanor

Ilkeston

Erewash

Derbyshire Dales and South Derbyshire

Derby City

Long Eaton

Swadlincote

Allestree Park Lake

Main Ave, Allestree, Derby.

SAT
DE22 2EG
NAV

Ticket Price: Day tickets are £4.30. Concessions at £2.15.

Directions: From Derby take the A52 Ashbourne Road. At the roundabout, take the 3rd exit onto Queensway/A38. At the next roundabout take the 2nd exit onto Duffield Road. Turn left after half a mile into Main Ave.

Description: A decent sized lake of about 7 acres. Set in a wonderful country park and situated next to an 18 hole golf course. Lots of carp ranging from 5 to high 20's. There is jack pike of around 6 - 7 lb. with the chance of catching a large pike, up to 30lb. Large bream and tench can be had when they are located. Boilies do well (as usual) for the carp. Maggots and pinkies for the silver fish. Bread and worms can catch good bags of bream with the occasional tench thrown in.

Types of Fish: Pike, perch, bream, chub, roach, carp and tench.

Rules/Bans: The fishing is Dawn till Dusk. Although no rules are listed, a sensible approach is advised.

Number of Lakes: One

Facilities:

Telephone: Park Ranger 01332 367 800

Sat Nav: DE22 2EG

Barlow Fishery

Barlow Trout and Coarse Fishery, Barlow.

SAT S18 7TJ NAV

Ticket Price: Coarse day ticket £5.00 After 1pm £4.00
Juniors, OAP's £4.00. Evening tickets £3.00.
Matches by arrangement.
Trout Lakes: Full day £19.00 four fish taken. £17.00 three fish taken. £15.00 two fish taken.

Directions: The fishery is located in the village of Barlow on the B6051, midway between Chesterfield and Owler Bar. Look out for the signs at the west end of the village.

Description: A great fishery for all ages and abilities with the last of the four lakes being most suitable for beginners. This well established fishery gives the angler plenty of choice with four coarse lakes and four trout lakes, plus a small brook. The four coarse lakes are stocked with a variety of fish with the largest carp being in the first two waters. The third pond is the tench pond and the last one is mixed. The cafe serves a great bacon sandwich.

Types of Fish: Carp, rudd, bream, tench, roach, trout, barbel, and chub.

Rules/Bans: Barbless hooks only , no keepnets,
no hard baits, no ground bait, no hemp.

Number of Lakes: Four coarse, four trout.   Sat Nav: S18 7TJ

Facilities: 2

Telephone: 0114 2890543

Beechwood Park

Main Road, Elvaston, Thulston, Derby.

Ticket Price: Day Ticket - Adult £5 Concessionary £3

Directions: Come off the A6 at Thulston Roundabout. Take the B5010. Turn third left, (this is still the B5010) go through the village, you will come to the park after approximately 1 mile.

Description: There are six lakes to fish at Beechwood Park. Warren Lake (some people refer to it as 'The Doughnut' because of its shape), is the oldest lake on the complex. With 24 pegs situated on an Island. Mature trees surround the lake, and lily pads and reed beds make for not only a picturesque setting, but also interesting fishing! Warren Lake is well stocked with big carp running to low double figures along with a good helping of smaller ones in the 2 - 5lb bracket. All other coarse fish can also be caught including roach to 1lb+, tench to 5lbs and bream to 4lbs.

Types of Fish: Carp, roach, rudd, tench, bream, chub and perch

Rules/Bans: Six baits are allowed. Maggots, casters, sweetcorn, luncheon meat, worms and bread - ALL OTHER BAITS ARE BANNED.
Barbless hooks must be used at all times.
Keepnets are only allowed in matches.

Number of Lakes: Six   **Sat Nav:** DE72 3EQ

Facilities:

Telephone: 01332 751938 or 07973 562689

3

Beehive Woodland Lakes

Lullington Road, Rosliston, Swadlincote,

SAT DE12 8JD NAV

Ticket Price: Day ticket (1 rod) £6.00 (2 rods) £10.00
Junior Day Ticket (1 rod only) £4.00. 11yrs and under.

Directions: Look for brown signs on Linton
Road. Access is from the A38 avoiding the
narrow bridge at Walton on Trent.

Description: Three well stocked lakes, The
Horseshoe, Botany Bay and new Jubilee
Lake are all popular with local fisherman.
The lakes are set in an attractive
woodland landscape. They provide an
ideal venue for a quiet day spent alone. Botany Bay Lake
has platforms suitable for disabled fishermen and easy
access from the nearby free car parking.

Types of Fish: The lakes are up to 12 feet in depth and stock
includes carp up to 26 lbs, tench up to 6 lbs, bream up to 4
lbs and roach up to 2 lbs. Rudd and perch are also present.

Rules/Bans: No nuts, boilies, pastes, pellets, bloodworm or
joker. Seeds: Only hemp and sweetcorn to be used.
Ground Bait: Only 1Kg maximum (dry weight) to be used.
No method feeding: Slip feeders only.
Barbless hooks only: Persons fishing with barbed hooks will
be asked to leave the lakes immediately. No Keepnets.
Landing Nets must be used.   **Sat Nav:** DE12 8JD

Number of Lakes: Three   **Telephone:** 01283 763981

Facilities:

Birch House Lakes

Derby Road, Ednaston, Brailsford, Ashbourne.

SAT **DE6 3AX** NAV

Ticket Price: Adults £6 per rod. OAP & Disabled £5.50 Juniors £5.00 per rod. Children under 14 must be accompanied by an adult at all times.

Directions: From the A38 travel south until you get to Park roundabout, then follow the A52 towards Ashbourne. Derby Lane can be found shortly after passing through Brailsford.

Description: There are now eight lakes totalling 12 acres of water. The fishery provides a mixture of pleasure and match angling on new and established waters.

There are plenty of car parking spaces, a fishing lodge where refreshments are available and modern facilities. The water bailiff is always on hand to offer help and advice.

I like to fish the more secluded Osprey Lake which is quite small at only three quarters of an acre. It's only got 14 pegs, and is very popular because of the large number of common and mirror carp.

This is a beautiful, tranquil spot on the outskirts of Ednaston.

Types of Fish: Roach, carp, bream, perch, tench and rudd.

Rules/Bans: No keepnets. Barbless hooks only. For other rules see sign at fishery.

Number of Lakes: Eight   **Sat Nav:** DE6 3AX

Facilities:

5

Telephone: 07796 874058

13

Bradleys Ponds

Geer Lane, Ford, Nr Sheffield.

Ticket Price: Day ticket £5.00. £3.00 after 4pm

Directions: From the A6102 Sheffield ring road at Gleadless turn onto White Lane signposted Mosborough. After a mile turn right to Ridgeway. Follow the road till you reach Ford. Turn left after the pub on the corner and continue up Geer Lane until you reach the farm. The ponds are on your left.

Description: There are three ponds to try. I prefer the middle one which is also the largest at around two acres.
This pond has a small island at one end which I fished up to using a 13 metre pole. I caught a few carp at an average weight of 8lb, plus plenty of silver fish. This is a popular fishery so it is advised to arrive early to get a good peg, the fishing is also much better early on at Bradleys. Set in an attractive valley of a working farm.

Types of Fish: Carp, bream, tench, perch, roach and rudd.

Rules/Bans: No carp in keepnets, No cereal ground baits except bread punch, barbless hooks only. No dogs.
No night fishing.

Number of Lakes: Three   Sat Nav: S12 3YH

Facilities: P   **Telephone:** 01246 435563

Butterley Reservoir
Butterley Hill, Ripley.

SAT DE5 3LT NAV

Ticket Price: Adult £5.00. Junior and Concessions £3.00. Full Membership £35.00. OAP Member £20.00. Junior Member £15.00.

Directions: Head out of Ripley towards Swanwick on the B6179. Continue down the hill. Shortly after the road bends to the right, look for the car park entrance on your left.

Description: This reservoir which is bisected by Midland Railway Societys steam train track is run by Ripley & District Angling Club. This 30 acre water is ideal for the serious carp or pike angler. The carp that reach 28lb are regularly caught with pop up boilies. Most of the 50 pegs are large and in good condition.

Types of Fish: Bream, tench, roach, perch, pike and carp.

Rules/Bans: See club rules on notice board.

PIKE FISHING RULES

1. PIKE FISHING IS PERMITTED ALL YEAR ROUND, BUT IS STRICTLY MEMBERS ONLY AT COPPICE LAKE.
2. JUNIOR ANGLERS MUST BE ACCOMPANIED BY A COMPETENT ADULT
3. ANGLERS MUST USE EQUIPMENT SUITABLE FOR HANDLING LARGE FISH ie LARGE LANDING NET FOR SPECIMEN FISH, UNHOOKING MAT, LONG FORCEPS, WIRE TRACES AND REEL LINES OF 12 LB (5.5KG) BREAKING STRAIN MINIMUM.
4. ALL FISH TO BE RETURNED ALIVE.
5. NO LIVE BAITS OVER 6" (15CM) TO BE USED.
6. NO CARP, TENCH OR BREAM TO BE USED AS LIVE BAIT.
7. NO LIVE BAITS TO BE TAKEN AWAY.
8. ONLY FISH CAUGHT ON THE WATER TO BE USED AS LIVE BAIT.
9. LIVE BAITS MUST BE KEPT IN KEEP NET OR LARGE BUCKET WITH AIR PUMP.
10. RODS MUST NOT BE LEFT UNATTENDED.

THE ABOVE RULES MUST BE STRICTLY ADHERRED TO.

Facilities:

Number of Lakes: One

Sat Nav: DE5 3LT to nearest houses.

Telephone: 01773 745837

7

Carr Vale Pond

Water Lane, Bolsover.

Ticket Price: Day tickets £4.00. Concessions / Evening £2.50

Carr Vale Pond

Description: Carr Vale is definitely worth a try. Its reputation for an excellent match pond is well foundered with good weights recorded most Sundays. Meaning pleasure anglers may want to give Sundays a miss. The pond is packed with most species of fish with a good head of carp and tench. The pond is a triangular shape, with the far bank being most popular, due to its shelter from the wind. A mixture of carp and pole fisherman were all catching well on my visit. It is advised to come early as it can get busy.

Facilities: ♿ P   **Sat Nav:** S44 6JP
to the top of the lane.   8

Rules/Bans: Keepnets only in matches. No night fishing. Barbless hooks only. No litter to be left. No fires. Ground bait in pole cup or feeder only.   **Telephone:** 01246 823477

Chesterfield Canal

Four sections across Chesterfield.

Ticket Price: Day Ticket are available from the Tapton Lock Visitors Centre or the bailiff on the bank.
Adult £3.00. Concessionary £2.00
Permit prices: Adult £20.00. Concessionary £10.00

Directions:
All venues.

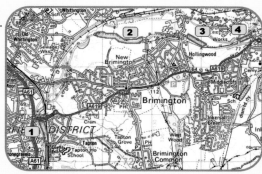

Description: Venue 1. Tapton Bridge to Tapton Lock Visitors Centre. 20 pleasure pegs available.
Access: The Tapton Lock Visitors Centre, off the Tesco roundabout on the A61 Chesterfield-Sheffield bypass or the A619 Brimington-Chesterfield (Rother Way)
Parking: Some on road parking available, near Tapton Lock visitors centre.

Types of Fish:
All four stretches of canal have roach, bream, carp, tench, chub, perch and gudgeon.

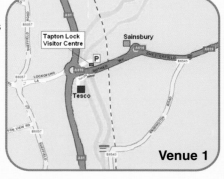

Venue 1

Rules/Bans: Barbless hooks only.

Telephone: 01246 472726 / 0775 3994439
BARROW HILL MEMORIAL ANGLING CLUB

Description: Venue 2. Bluebank Lock to Dixon's Lock.
1-20 above Bilby Lane Bridge, 21-57 below (Total 57)
Access: Use the public footpath behind the Ringwood Day Centre, Station Road, Hollingwood.
Please note Bilby Lane is closed to all vehicles.
Parking: Some off road parking available, behind the Ringwood Day Centre.

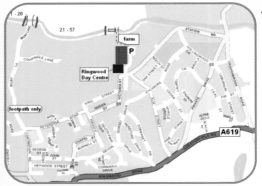

Venue 2

Description: Venue 3. Hollingwood Lock to Mill Green.
No. of pegs : 58-83 (26)
Access: Use the towpath down stream off Hollingwood Lock, Works Road.
Parking: Some on road parking available, near Hollingwood Lock on Works Road.

Venue 3

Description: Venue 4. Mill Green.
No. of pegs : 84-100 (17)
Access: Use the small road branching off from the entrance to Morrisons car park, Staveley.
Parking: Some on road parking available, near Morrisons.

Venue 4

Codnor Park Fisheries

Coach Road, Codnor Park.

SAT NG16 5PX NAV

Ticket Price: Day Tickets £4.00. Concessions £2.00.

Directions: From Ripley take the A610 Nottingham Road. After one and a half miles turn sharp left at Alfreton Road. Continue onto Codnor Lane. After a mile turn right onto Coach Road. Continue until you see the reservoir on your left.

Description: On the border of Derbyshire and Nottinghamshire this natural nine acre reservoir offers something for both the novice angler and the more experienced match fisherman. Great tench pole fishing tight to the many reed beds near most pegs. Sweetcorn or meat are the baits to use for both the tench and few carp that are present. Many anglers were also using a feeder rod to catch the good head of bream that can be found in the deeper water. Matches are held on Sundays but you can still find one of the 46 pegs to pleasure fish from.

Types of Fish: Tench, roach, bream, crucian carp, perch and a few carp.

Rules/Bans: Barbless hooks only. No keepnets except for matches.

Number of Lakes: One

Facilities: 10

Telephone: 07941 824374   **Sat Nav:** NG16 5PX

Coopers Lake

Off Weston Road, Weston On Trent, Derby.

Ticket Price: £6 during the day and £4 for the evening.

Directions: Come off the A50 and head for Aston-on-Trent. Just before you enter the town turn right and follow the signs for Weston-on-Trent. Once in the village turn right by the Coopers Arms. The lake is within the grounds of the Pub.

Description: Coopers Lake is a beautifully matured 5 acre lake, fully stocked in order to satisfy all levels of anglers expertise. Anglers who can choose to fish from either natural or constructed pegs. If you are a pleasure angler, it could not be simpler, just arrive, check the notice boards, decide on your peg and the bailiff will issue you with a day ticket. This is a delightful venue which is packed with quality fish. Refreshments can be ordered for delivery to the bank. How good is that!

Types of Fish: The fish stock comprises of Roach, tench, bream, barbel, crucian and common carp (some of which are up to double figures).

Number of Lakes: One

Facilities:

Rules/Bans:
See Notice board

Sat Nav: DE72 2BJ

Telephone: Tel: 01332 665574   Mob: 07976 982081   11

Dunston Park Farm

Dunston Road, Chesterfield.

SAT S41 9RW NAV

Ticket Price: Yearly ticket, two rods £150. Runs from date of purchase.

Directions: Leave Chesterfield heading towards Sheffield on the A61. Come off at the first junction, turn left and immediate left again on to Sheepbridge Lane. Follow the road to the top and turn right onto Dunston Road. Continue along Dunston Road for approximately 1.5 miles until you see the farm on your right hand side.

Description: This secluded 1½ acre lake has a small island in the middle and is fully stocked with specimen fish. It's open to individuals, families and fishing clubs. The lake is open 12 months of the year. It's well stocked with mirror carp, common carp, ghost carp, grass carp, roach, perch, bream, rudd and tench and is known to contain fish in excess of 30lbs. Try fishing up to the island for the carp. Depths vary from four feet at one end to eight feet at the far side.

Rules/Bans: No keepnets, barbless hooks only.

Number of Lakes: One   **Sat Nav:** S41 9RW

Facilities:

Telephone: 01246 237186

Erewash Canal (Long Eaton)

Long Eaton Lock down to Trent Lock.

Ticket Price: Day ticket price £2.50

Directions: The Canal runs adjacent to the Tamworth Road, Long Eaton, and may be accessed at any point between the Fire Station and Canal Bridge. Park, where permitted, along the Tamworth Road or any of the side roads leading off it, or behind the 'Old Ale House' pub (after seeking permission).

Description: There are large fish throughout this stretch, most of the biggest specimens are taken from the Trent Lock end, with the exception of the big perch which show throughout the whole length. Pole tactics are most popular, although rod and line (with waggler) can also produce, as can ledgering for the big carp which take corn and meat. Other successful baits are, maggots, squats or pinkies, casters, hemp, tares, worms and bread. The fish will respond to both loose feed and groundbait in moderation.

Types of Fish: This is an excellent canal fishery, and contains the following species: Roach (to 1lb), perch (to 3½lb), chub (to 6lb), bream (to 5lb), gudgeon, tench, carp and pike (to 20lb).

Rules/Bans:
Fishing is only permitted from permanently marked pegs.
Live baiting on this canal stretch is strictly prohibited.

Telephone: 0115 972 8547
Long Eaton Victoria Angling Society.

Erewash Canal (Sandiacre)
Sandiacre Bridge to Stanton Lock, Derbyshire.

Ticket Price: Nottingham Anglers Association run this stretch of canal. The Membership fees are: Full Member £39.00. Disabled or over 65 £29.00. Juniors (under 15) £9.00. Day tickets are £3.00. Concessions £1.50.

Directions: From the A6002 Coventry Lane continue past Bramcote Crematorium down to the mini roundabout, turn right and continue straight on along Ilkeston Road for ½ mile to a mini roundabout and turn left into Pasture Road. Travel 200 Yards along Pasture Road and turn right into Moorbridge Lane. Continue for 750 Yards and go over the railway bridge, just over the railway the canal passes under the road. This is Stanton Gate Bridge, there is a small parking area on the right. To get to Sandiacre continue along this road to a T Junction and turn left into Ilkeston Road and continue for ¾ mile along this road into Town Street, Mill Lane is on the left.

Description: This section of the Erewash Canal runs from the road bridge in Sandiacre Town to Stanton Lock, a distance of just over 1½ miles. At the Sandiacre end the area is quite urban with houses and factory buildings on the opposite bank, however, this does not detract from the good fishing on offer with roach, bream, chub and perch being present all year round. Further up the canal it opens up into pleasant countryside before reaching Pasture Lock. The area below the lock is known locally as 'Sandy Bottoms' and is highly regarded for skimmers. From Pasture Lock the canal then heads towards Stanton Gate before going under the motorway and railway and on to Stanton Lock.

Rules/Bans: Barbless hooks. No night fishing.

Telephone: 0115 919 9500   **Sat Nav:** NG10 5DT   14

Hall Farm Fishery

Sutton Lane, Sutton Scarsdale, Chesterfield.

SAT S44 5UW NAV

Ticket Price: Day ticket £5.00. Concessions £3.00. Half day £3.00

Directions: From junction 29 of the M1 take the dual carriage way heading towards Chesterfield. Come off at the first exit and turn right. Follow the B6425 until it meets the A632 and turn right. After a few yards turn right onto Sutton Lane. Follow the lane for about a mile, you will see the signpost for the fishery on your left.

Description: This new fishery consists of two small ponds. The first pond you see is the largest of the two and surprisingly holds quite a few large fish. While I was setting up, a pole angler nearby hooked into something that took his elastic from one side of the pond to the other. It snapped his hook length so neither of us saw what fish it was. Great when there's no wind but is very exposed when there is a breeze.

Types of Fish: Recently stocked with carp, roach, perch, ide, bream, tench and crucian carp.

Rules/Bans:

Number of Lakes: Two

Facilities: ♿ P

Sat Nav: S44 5UW

Telephone: 07836 226276

HALL FARM FISHERY

1. BARBLESS HOOKS ONLY
2. MAXIMUM HOOK SIZE 12
3. CARP FRIENDLY NETS
4. DO NOT ROLL FISH DOWN NETS
5. TINS MUST NOT BE VISIBLE ON BANKSIDE
6. GROUNDBAIT FED IN FEEDER OR POLECUP ONLY
7. FEEDERS MUST BE FREE RUNNING
8. NO LITTER
9. KEEP NETS ONLY TO BE USED ON MATCH DAYS

BAITS

1. MAGGOTS
2. CASTERS
3. WORMS
4. PELLETS (NO TROUT PELLETS)
5. SWEETCORN (1 SMALL TIN PER ANGLER)
6. LUNCHEON MEAT (1 SMALL TIN PER ANGLER)
7. NO FLOATING BAITS
8. NO FLOATING POLES

THESE RULES ARE IN FORCE TO CREATE A FISHERY FOR THE FUTURE AND ARE LIABLE TO CHANGE

Hardwick Park Ponds

Hardwick Hall, near Holmewood, Derbyshire.

SAT NAV S44 5QJ

Ticket Price: £5.00 per rod for day or night fishing. Season permits are £50.00 for one rod or £100 for three rods. Season runs from 16th June to 28th February.

Directions: From the M1 Junction 29, take the A6175 heading towards Holmewood. Take your first left onto Mill lane. Continue along this road that runs parallel to the M1. Follow the signs to Hardwick Hall. Turn left into the park immediately after the road goes under the motorway.

Description: Two great waters to try. The first pond you will see is Great Pond, this has a dam wall running along one edge. You can fish this stretch but you can get a lot of walkers passing your swim. Try fishing the other end, its a bit quieter. Saying that, you can always hear the drown of the motorway in the distance. Most anglers that fish both these ponds are going for the carp which reach 20lb. There are also plenty of good sized tench, chub, pike and bream.

Types of Fish:

Number of Lakes: Two

Rules/Bans: There are general and carp fishing regulations for both ponds available from the visitors centre that is situated between the ponds.

Facilities: ♿ 🚻 ☕ 🅿️   16

Telephone: 01246 851787   **Sat Nav:** S44 5QJ

Harlesthorpe Dam

Rotherham Road, Clowne.

Ticket Price: Smaller pond £5.00. Concessions £4.00 Large Dam £6.00. Concessions £5.00. Extra Rod £1.00. Night fishing on island only, £15.00 ring for details.

Directions: From the M1 take the A619 to Clowne. At the crossroad in the centre of Clowne turn left onto the A618. The fishery is a few hundred yards, on both sides of the road.

Description: The main lake of about 10 acres is mainly stocked with carp up to 25lb, and with plenty over 10lb you are sure of good net weights. The depth can vary from 5 feet in the reeds to 14 feet in the middle. I prefer the smaller lake across the road that is surrounded by trees and has a variety of fish present, with good sized chub and tench.

Types of Fish: Carp, tench, chub, roach, bream, perch, rudd and crucian carp.

Rules/Bans: Barbless hooks only. Children under 16 years of age must be accompanied by an adult. No dogs or radios permitted. Carp over 3lb exempt from keep nets (except for matches). No method feeder. No dog or cat meat allowed. Ground bait in pole or cup feeder only.

Facilities: **Sat Nav:** S43 4PS   17

Telephone: 01246 810231   **Number of Lakes:** Two

Higham Farm Fishery

Main Road, Higham.

SAT NAV DE55 6EH

Ticket Price: Day Ticket £8.00 per person per day. £20.00 for 24 hours.

Directions: Follow the A61 out of Chesterfield. When you reach Higham the road bends to the left, turn right here on to Main Road. After 300 yrds turn right at Santo's Hotel. Follow the sign to the fishing on your left. This takes you down a lane to the ponds.

Description: A bit pricey at eight pounds but the quality of the fish is outstanding. Three out of the four ponds are quite deep and are more suited to the carp angler. One of which is a specimen carp lake and can only be fished on a 24 hour ticket. I chose the water second on the right. This has plenty of lilies to fish up to, which suits the pole angler. I caught mainly silver fish and a couple of small carp on sweetcorn. When I switched to pellet a caught a tench at around 5lbs. All the ponds have plenty of carp over 8lb as you can see from the photo.

Types of Fish:

Sat Nav:
DE55 6EH   **Number of Lakes:** Four

Rules/Bans: Barbless hooks only, no nuts or boiled seeds One lake is 24 hrs only. See other rules on site.

Telephone: 01773 602741   **Facilities:**

Holymoorside Dam

Loads Road, Holymoorside, Chesterfield.

SAT NAV S42 7ET

Ticket Price: Day Tickets are not available. Membership cards can be bought from Leegem Angling, Chesterfield or from Climax Fishing Tackle, Dronfield. Full Membership (16yrs and over) £15.00 Per Year (£7.00 Joining fee first year.) Junior (12yrs to 15yrs) and OAP £7.00 Per Year (£3.00 Joining Fee first year.)
Juveniles under 12yrs are free but must obtain a membership book and must be accompanied by an adult.

Directions: Head out of Chesterfield on the A619 Chatsworth Road. Turn left onto Holymoor Road. At the junction at Holymoorside Village turn left and you will see the pond on your right.

Description: The venue is approximately 1.7 acres in size with an average depth of about two and a half feet. The venue contains carp to around 18lb, tench to 6lb, chub to 2lb, bream to 6lb and roach and perch. In early spring tench can be caught on pellet with chopped worm and caster also catching well all year round. The best nets of fish can be caught fishing under near bank trees or close to the island.

Rules/Bans: No keepnets. Barbless hooks only.

Number of Lakes: One

Facilities:

Telephone: 01246 232058
Holymoorside Angling Club

Sat Nav: S42 7ET

Kilburn Lake

Killis Lane, Kilburn, Belper.

Ticket Price: Day Tickets £6.00. Concessions £5.00. Purchased from the bailiff on the bank.

Directions: From the village of Kilburn stay on the B609 to Belper, approximately one mile from Kilburn turn left into Killis Lane, almost immediately turn right for the lake (signposted). Follow the roadway up the hill to the lake and car park.

Description: Margin fishing or surface baits are popular methods in the summer. Fishing at 8 metres on the bottom was very effective in the cooler months. Pellets, paste and bread work well from any of the 28 pegs as does sweetcorn and meat baits. Carp to 8lb, many fish averaging 1-2lb, with roach and bream for variety. Set in picturesque countryside this venue offers excellent fishing for the beginner or experienced angler alike.

Types of Fish: Carp, roach and bream, plus various other silver fish.

Rules/Bans: Barbed hooks banned at all times. Keepnets banned except in organised matches. Open from dawn to dusk. NO NIGHT FISHING.

Number of Lakes: One

Facilities:

Telephone: 01473 327366   **Sat Nav:** DE56 0LS

Loscoe Dam

Furnace Lane, Loscoe, Heanor.

Ticket Price: This water is run by NCB Area No.5 Fishing Club. Season Tickets from June 16th to June 15th each year. Seniors £27.00. Concessionary £21.00. Senior Citizens £12.00. Intermediate (16-17 years old) £17.00. Juniors £7.00. Night Fishing for adults (additional) £8.00 Day tickets are available (cost per rod) £3.00

Directions:

Description: Loscoe dam is a good pond but very shallow and weedy. It has some large carp a lot of good size crucian, plenty of tench and some very small carp at only a few ounces. I took my younger brother of age 8 along with me who thoroughly enjoyed catching these small carp on a 3 metre whip, size 18 hook and a single maggot, while I fished for the crucian and tench. A very enjoyable summer venue. (Fishing review by Ed Heath).

Types of Fish: Carp up to 18lb, tench to 4lb, crucians to 2lb, roach to 2lb. and a few bream are present.

Facilities: **Number of Lakes:** One
Sat Nav: DE75 7LT

Rules/Bans: Barbless hooks only. **Telephone:** 07966 871 623

Manor Floods

Manners Ave, Manners Ind Est, Ilkeston.

SAT DE7 8YA NAV

Ticket Price: Day Tickets £3.00
Season tickets are available at the following rates:
Seniors £27.00. Concessionary £21.00
Senior Citizens £12.00. Intermediate (16-17 years old)
£17.00. Juniors £7.00. Night Fishing for adults (additional)
£8.00. Season Tickets from June 16th to June 15th.

Directions:

Description: This water is about 5 acres and very weedy.
The lake holds many carp in the 20lb bracket. Best carp
method used are boilie with PVA bags of pellets. In the
summer months floating baits are quite productive. Pike go
to 28lb, dead bait and live bait work equally well and plugs
are good for Jack Pike. The water isn't very deep, maximum
depth of about 7 or 8 feet. This water is closed from 15th
March until 16th June as it still carries its closed season.

Types of Fish: The water is stocked with carp, pike, tench and
a solitary bream at about 12lb, crucian carp, gudgeon, chub
and roach make up the other species.

Number of Lakes: One

Facilities:
None

Sat Nav:
DE7 8YA

Telephone: NCB Area No 5 Fishing Club, 07966 871 623

Mapperly Reservoir
Shipley Lane, Ilkeston, Derbyshire.

SAT NAV DE7 6BR

Ticket Price: Day Tickets £3.00
Season tickets are available at the following rates:
Seniors £27.00. Concessionary £21.00
Senior Citizens £12.00. Intermediate (16-17 years old)
£17.00. Juniors £7.00. Night Fishing for adults (additional)
£8.00. Season Tickets from June 16th to June 15th.

Directions:

Description: This reservoir is well run by NCB Area 5 Fishing Club. This water is around 21 acres. The depth averages 14 to 18 feet off the dam wall. The carp in this water go to Mid 20`s with the biggest caught up to now at 26lb. Many anglers who fish this water cast towards the middle where they catch most of the larger carp but a few can be caught in the margins as well. In the summer you get pestered by tench averaging about 4lb. The reservoir is stocked with carp, pike, tench, bream, perch, gudgeon and roach.

Number of Lakes: One   **Sat Nav:** DE7 6BR

Facilities: ♿   **Rules/Bans:** Available on site.   23

Telephone: NCB Area No 5 Fishing Club, 07966 871 623

McGregors Pond

McGregors Way, Chesterfield.

Ticket Price: Day ticket £3.00. Extra rod £1.00. Concessions £2.00. Night ticket £10.00. Full season permit £40.00. Day season permit £25.00.

Directions: Head out of Chesterfield City centre on the A61 Derby Road. After only a mile turn left onto Storforth Lane. Take the second right into Burley Close. Drive through the industrial estate and turn right onto Mcgregors Way. The car park is between two industrial units.

Description: This very attractive, hidden away pond on the edge of Chesterfield is run by McGregors Angling Club. It's around two acres and has reed beds, lily pads and patches of bullrushes to fish up to. The small island in the middle can be reached with a long pole from half a dozen of the 29 pegs available. There are some good sized carp in this pond, well into double figures. Floating baits are not banned but there are a lot of ducks and geese around, so be careful.

Types of Fish: Bream, tench, roach, perch and carp.

Rules/Bans: See club rules on notice board.

Number of Lakes: One   **Sat Nav:** S40 2WB

Facilities: **Telephone:** 0772 5987053

Meadow Park Pond
Newmarket Lane, Clay Cross.

Ticket Price: Day tickets £5. Year permit £15 from Clay Cross Angling, High Street, Clay Cross.

Directions: Head out of Chesterfield on the A61. At the traffic lights at Clay Cross turn right onto Clay Lane. Take your second right into Newmarket Lane. Look for a turning on the right after 1/4 mile. The pond is at the end of the lane.

Description: This lake is run by Clay Cross Angling Association and is very well kept. There are plenty of good sized pegs for the carp angler to set up two rods. Most anglers were targeting the carp over twenty pounds. The margins close to the large island in the centre seemed the obvious choice to fish. Well worth a visit if you also want to catch a few big pike.

Types of Fish: Large carp, perch, chub, tench, bream, roach and some good sized pike.

Rules/Bans:

FISHING DAWN UNTIL DUSK ONLY.
NO CARP IN KEEPNETS OVER 5lb.
ONE ROD PER DAY TICKET.
MAXIMUM OF TWO RODS.
LANDING NETS TO BE USED AT ALL TIMES.
NO FISH TO BE TAKEN FROM POND.
NO WADING.
1Kg BOILIES PER SESSION.
PLEASE REMOVE ALL LITTER.

Facilities: ♿ 🅿

Telephone: 01245 251777
Clay Cross Angling

Sat Nav: S45 9AP

Number of Lakes: One

Osborne's Pond

Roper Avenue, Heanor, Derbyshire.

SAT **DE75 7BZ** NAV

Ticket Price: Day Tickets £3.00
Season tickets are available at the following rates:
Seniors £27.00. Concessionary £21.00
Senior Citizens £12.00. Intermediate (16-17 years old)
£17.00. Juniors £7.00. Night Fishing for adults (additional)
£8.00. Season Tickets from June 16th to June 15th.

Directions:

Description: Osborne's pond is situated in Shipley Park and is almost 7 acres. Most anglers fish for the carp which run to the mid 20's. It's also popular for the roach, tench and bream as stocks are very high in this water. The best method is to float fish with bread but many carp do fall to boilie. It's a great tench fishing venue with many reaching 6lb. The only downfall is the amount of people walking nearby as this is a very busy area of the Park but the fish are used to the noise and can still be caught in the margins.

Types of Fish: This water is stocked with carp, tench, pike, bream, crucian carp, roach, perch, gudgeon, chub and a few barbel

Rules/Bans: Do not leave rods unattended. Dogs must be kept under control. No litter. No fires. If carp or pike fishing, unhooking mats are required.

Sat Nav:
DE75 7BZ

Lakes:
One

Facilities:

26

Telephone: NCB Area No 5 Fishing Club, 07966 871 623

Poolsbrook Country Park

Erin Road, Poolsbrook, Chesterfield.

SAT NAV S43 3WL

Ticket Price: Day Tickets £3.50
Adult Permits £25 - £20 after first year.
Concessions £15 -£10 after first year.

Directions: From the Tesco roundabout on the A61, head towards Brimington. Go through Brimington and take Ringwood Road, this turns into Chesterfield Road. Follow this road into the centre of Staveley. Turn right at the lights onto Inkersall Road. Take your second left into Cemetery Lane. Turn right at the T junction. Follow the road for a short distance until you see the lakes.

Description: Four ponds to try here, the largest called Markham is the most popular. I was reliably told Markham Lake has bream to 7lb, blue orfe and golden tench. I prefer one of the smaller lakes called Island Lake. This pond has plenty of good sized carp in it, the largest around 21lb. Other species present are bream, roach, rudd, and the odd pike. The pegs are all new, if a bit close together. Very good flat access for disabled anglers.

Number of Lakes: Four

Rules/Bans: See notice board at the entrance.

Facilities: 27

Telephone: 01246 474423   Sat Nav: S43 3WL
Ireland Colliery Poolsbrook Fishing Club.

Press Manor Fishery

Bolehill Lane, Old Tupton, Nr Chesterfield.

Ticket Price: Day Ticket £5.00, 2 rods £6.50. Concessions £4.50. Night fishing (24 hr ticket) £12.00. (Contact the owner to book night fishing)

Directions: Take the A61 out of Chesterfield. At the first roundabout turn right onto Nethermoor Road. At the next roundabout take the second exit. Then take your second left onto Birkin Lane. Take your next left and follow the lane until you see the fishery on your right.

Description: This triangular shaped lake is around 3 acres. The pegs near the car park are the deepest but I wanted to fish the margins at the far end where the depth is around 3 feet. The fish were spawning on the day I chose so it was slow going. Saying that I must have caught well over 30 skimmer bream, a couple of large roach and a 2lb barbel. Pellet and paste were the best bait with a bed of micro pellets to attract the fish. The carp that go to 20lb show to floating crust or dog biscuit in the summer months. Fly fishing is also available on the other lake.

Types of Fish: The lake is stocked with roach, bream, carp, barbel, and tench.

Rules/Bans:

Rules

- Take all your litter home.
- Treat all fish with respect-do not drop them on concrete platforms.
- All fish to be returned.
- For fish welfare No Keep-nets to be used MAY to AUGUST inclusive. (No Carp species are to be put in Keep-nets at any time)
- Release fish from Keep-nets carefully.
- Bait Bans: Blood-Worm, Joker, Tiger-nuts and Peanuts.
- Do not bring disease onto our water, ensure Landing nets and Keep-nets are dry before fishing.
- Night fishing must be booked in advance-Phone Bernie or Brian.
- No responsibility is taken by the owner, for loss or damage to equipment, person or vehicles howsoever caused.
- When we have matches we will indicate which pegs are available for pleasure fishing.

Telephone: 07976 306073

Number of Lakes: One + one game fishing lake

Facilities: P Sat Nav: S42 6AZ

28

Ringwood Lake

Chesterfield Road A619, Staveley.

Ticket Price: Day tickets and year permits have to be purchased before fishing from Cliff Madden tackle shop in Staveley. Day tickets £2.50. Adult Permit £15.00 (2 rods) Concessions £10.00 (2 rods).

Directions: From the Tesco roundabout on the A61, head towards Brimington. Go through Brimington and take Ringwood Road, this turns into Chesterfield Road. After about one mile, turn right at the bottom of the hill onto Inkersall Green Road. As soon as you turn you will see the car park for the park. The lake is at the end of the car park.

Description: This is a good sized park lake that has plenty of well kept pegs. It can be fished with a pole to about 10 metre for most silver fish. The anglers that I spoke to were serious carp fisherman who had there bivvies up to shelter from the rain. They were going for the 20lb+ commons that are present. The lake is about four acres so be prepared for a long walk from your car. security of your car is also a bit of a worry.

Types of Fish: Carp, tench, roach, perch and bream.

Rules/Bans: Barless Hooks only.

Number of Lakes: One

Facilities:

Telephone: 01246 472410 Cliff Madden Tackle Shop.

Sat Nav: Not available

Robinwood Lakes

Off Ingleby Road, Swarkstone, Derby.

Ticket Price: Please ring Chris Murfin to enquire about fishing the lakes and booking for matches.
07876 576927 Mornings. 01332 727875 Evenings.

Directions: From the M1 Junction 24, take the A50. Come off the A50 at Junction 3 and head to Swarkstone. Turn left in Swarkstone and cross the River Trent. As soon as you cross the river turn right. Follow the road past the gravel pits and take your second right. Follow the lane to the lakes.

Description: I fished Pond Two on a hot spring day and really enjoyed it. Even though I missed a few good bites, I did manage to catch six carp all between 7-12lb. There are a few very big fish in this pond, one of which took my bait and steamed off across the pond, snapping my 8lb hook length easily. Pond One has mainly silver fish, pond Two and Three have the larger carp. Pond Four is the more mature pond and contains a mix of silver fish and carp. This fishery is well run by Shardlow Angling Club.

Types of Fish: Tench to 9lb, bream to 14lb, Large common and mirror carp, roach, perch, rudd, barbel and chub.

30

Facilities: ♿ 🚻 P ☕   Sat Nav: DE73 7HT to nearest house.

Rules/Bans: See ticket supplied.   **Number of Lakes:** Four

Telephone: 07976 576927 Mornings. 01332 727875 Evenings.

Rycroft Fishery

Rycroft Road, Hemington.

Ticket Price: Day tickets £6.00. Extra rods £3.00

Directions: From the M1 - Junction 24 take the A50. After approximately one mile, exit at Junction 1 and turn immediate left onto Rycroft Road. After 1/2 a mile you will see the fishery on your left.

Description: Make sure you take pellets to this venue during the summer months as most species seem to feed well on them. Paste also works well. During the cooler months maggots will produce large weights of rudd. There are plenty of good sized carp in the new Canal Lake which love luncheon meat. Nets of over 100lb are no exaggeration. The Moat Lake has a sunken island in the middle, try floating baits for the carp. This is a very popular match fishery so check before setting off that there are some pleasure pegs available.

Types of Fish: Carp, bream, barbel, tench, roach, rudd, and chub.

Number of Lakes: Four

Facilities:

Rules/Bans: Barbless hooks. No keepnets except in matches.

Telephone: 07816 052235 or 07971 631537

Sat Nav: DE74 2RE

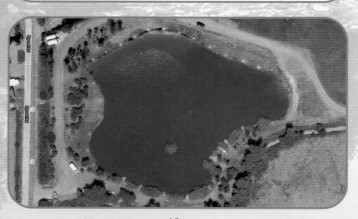

Shirebrook Town Pond

Park Road, Shirebrook.

Ticket Price: £2.00 adult. £1.00 concessions.
Season permit £12.00 adult. £6.00 concessions.

Directions: From J29, M1 take the A617 to Pleasley roundabout. Take the second exit for Shirebrook and follow all the signs for Kissingate Leisure Centre. The pond is behind the centre.

Description: Run by Shirebrook Angling Club, this disabled friendly pond is ideal for the new angler to the sport. There are even NFA coaches available. The pond is only 5 feet at its deepest and is most suited to float fishing a single maggot over some micro pellets. Caster or corn works well in the warmer months. Youngsters using a short whip were pulling out plenty of fish all around the pond. Great day's entertainment for £1.

Types of Fish: Carp, roach, tench, orfe, crucian, rudd, bream and perch.

Rules/Bans: Barbless hooks only. No keepnets.

Number of Lakes: One

Facilities: 🅿 🍔 🚻 ♿ 　32

Telephone: 07901 834765　　　　**Sat Nav:** NG20 8JQ

Shortheath Water

Shortheath Road, Moira, Swadlincote.

Ticket Price: Day Tickets £5.00. concession £4.00.
Use of a keepnet £1.00

Directions: From Ashby-de-la-Zouch head west on Moira
Road for one and a half miles. Continue onto Ashby Road
for another mile and straight over the roundabout. Continue
straight onto Shortheath Road and look out for the fishery
which is half a mile down the road on your left.

Description: Shortheath water is a 24 peg privately owned
lake set in about 4 acres of land. The Lake is mainly stocked
with carp, some weighing up to 20lbs. There are many
smaller fish including rudd, roach, tench and bream which
provide an added attraction. Situated at the front of the lake
are three disabled pegs (1, 2 and 3) which are adjacent to
the car park.

Types of Fish:

Rules/Bans: Barbless hooks only, no braided lines allowed.
The use of bread, ground bait (including feeder), biscuits,
boilies, jokers, peanuts, beans, chickpeas, tiger nuts, hemp
and seed baits, trout pellets and bloodworm are strictly
prohibited. Please do not use any floating baits.

Number of Lakes: One   **Telephone:** 01283 763777

Facilities:

Lakeside Lodge
accommodation
available.

Sat Nav: DE12 6BN

Sowbrook Lake

Sowbrook Lane, Kirk Hallam, Derbyshire.

Ticket Price: Membership of the Nottingham Anglers Association is required for this water. The Membership fees are: Full Member £39.00. Disabled or over 65 £29.00. Juniors (under 15) £9.00.

Directions: From M1 Junction 26 follow the A6002 towards Stapleford, continue along this road through two sets of traffic lights and past Bramcote Crematorium. At the end of this road turn right at the mini roundabout. Go straight on at the next mini roundabout and left at the next (this will be signposted Stapleford). Take the second turn on the right into Moorbridge Lane and continue along this lane to a T junction. Turn right and go under the motorway, continue along this road for approx 1 mile until you reach a sharp right hand bend, on this bend turn left (actually going straight on) the pond is on the right after approx 1/2 mile.

Description: A scheme lasting two years was carried out to reduce the depth by infilling with inert material (soil, clay, etc.) this also allowed the re-profiling of the banks to create a better fishing environment. The reduced depth that now averages 7ft has seen a good increase in fish catches with bream, roach, tench and carp the predominant species. Construction of six specially designed pegs suitable for wheelchair users, these along with stone paths and very good parking have made Sowbrook Lake ideal for disabled anglers.

 34

Number of Lakes: One   **Facilities:** P ♿   **Telephone:** 0115 919 9500

43

Springwood Fisheries

Ashby Road, Melbourne.

SAT NAV DE73 8BJ

Ticket Price: Adult £6.00. Concessions £4.00.

Directions: Situated on the B587 Ashby Road, in between Lount and Melbourne. It's easily accessible from the M1 & M42 using junction 13 of the A42 (signposted Ashby-de-la-Zouch).

Description: The two lakes are fed by natural spring water. They are both similar in size and depth and each have two islands to fish up to. The 24 peg Top Lake holds a large head of crucian carp and plenty of common, mirror and ghost carp between 6 and 14lbs. The 30 peg Bottom Lake has large numbers of Ide and other silver fish.

Types of Fish: Both lakes are stocked with Common Carp, Mirror Carp, Ghost Carp and other species such as Tench, Perch, Golden Orfe, Rudd, Roach and Skimmer Bream, barbel, ide, chub.

Rules/Bans: No keep nets (unless in organised matches). No night fishing. Barbless hooks only. No meat based pet food. No bloodworm or joker. No boilies or tiger nuts. No trout pellets. No floating bait or floating bread.

Number of Lakes: Two   **Sat Nav:** DE73 8BJ

Facilities: 35

Telephone: Tel: 01332 864331   Mobile: 07920 408062

Stonedge Ponds

Belland Lane, Nr Chesterfield.

SAT S45 0LN NAV

Ticket Price: Day Tickets are not available. Membership cards can be bought from Leegem Angling, Chesterfield or from Climax Fishing Tackle, Dronfield. Full Membership (16yrs and over) £15.00 Per Year (£7.00 Joining fee first year.) Junior (12yrs to 15yrs Incls) and OAP £7.00 Per Year (£3.00 Joining Fee first year.)
Juveniles under 12yrs are free but must obtain a membership book and must be accompanied by an adult.

Directions: Head out of Chesterfield on the A619 Chatsworth Road. Turn left onto the A632. Follow this road until you reach a right turn just before the Three Horseshoes pub. This is Belland Lane, the ponds are down a track on your left.

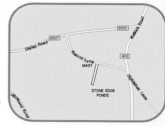

Description: The Island pond is the first pond reached from the track and contains carp to 18lb, tench to 5lb, perch to 2lb, plus roach and rudd. It is well stocked and fish can be caught tight to the island or under the near bank cover. The Strip Pond at Stonedge is situated at the end of the track at the side of the Island pond. The pond is approximately 100m long and contains mostly Carp to 6lb.

Rules/Bans: No keepnets. Barbless hooks only. **36**

Number of Lakes: Two   **Facilities:** None   **Sat Nav:** S45 0LN

Telephone: 01246 232058 Holymoorside Angling Club

Weston Moat Fishery

The Green, Weston on Trent, Derby.

SAT NAV DE72 2BJ

Ticket Price: Day Tickets £5.00 - 1 rod. £6.00 - 2 rods £8.00 - 3 rods. 24 Hour Ticket £15.00. Up to 3 rods £25.00

Directions: Come off the A50 and head for Aston-on-Trent. Just before you enter the town turn right and follow the signs for Weston-on-Trent. Once in the village turn right by the Coopers Arms. The fishery is on your right.

Description: This 2.5 acre lake has several carp over 20lbs and a good head of other coarse fish including roach, tench, bream, rudd and even ghost and koi carp. There are several ornamental fish like golden orfe, blue orfe and golden tench. The largest carp weighed in at 37.5 lbs. It only comes out once a year and was last was caught with a popped up worm over a bed of cockles!

Types of Fish: Tench, bream, rudd, roach, carp, orfe.

Rules/Bans: True Barbless hooks only. No cat or dog meat. No tiger or peanuts. Fishery boilies only. No fires. Dogs must be kept under control. All carp to be landed with a landing net. Unhooking mats must be used. Keepnets are allowed for fish 3lbs and under. Under 16's must be accompanied by an adult.

Facilities: ♿ 🅿 🚻   **Number of Lakes:** One

Telephone: 07815 097333   **Sat Nav:** DE72 2BJ   37

46

Williamthorpe Ponds

Mansfield Road, Holmewood, Chesterfield.

Ticket Price: Day tickets £5.00. Permits are available: New members £42. Senior £32. Juniors £16.

Directions: Come off the M1 at Junction 29 and take the A6175. Turn first right onto Main Street and follow the road for about one mile. The road becomes Mansfield Road. You will see the water on your left hand side.

Description: Williamthorpe Angling Club run these three ponds which are set within a nature reserve. Pond One next to the road has a mixture of silver fish, with some reasonable sized carp and barbel. The depth varies from four foot to six foot at the car park end. The other two ponds are bigger and hold the larger carp. These lakes are fished by the serious carp anglers who put there bivvies up for a few days at a time.

Rules/Bans: See notice board on site. **Sat Nav:** Not available

Number of Lakes: Three   **Telephone:** 01246 856977

Facilities: Car park over looking Pond One.

38

Wingerworth Lido

Nethermoor Rd, Wingerworth, Nr Chesterfield.

SAT NAV S42 6NL

Ticket Price: Day tickets £5. Year permit £15 from Clay Cross Angling, High Street, Clay Cross.

Directions: Come out of Chesterfield on the A61. After approximately one mile turn right onto Nethermoor Road at a small roundabout. Follow this road for a mile and you will see the lake on your right hand side.

Description: The lake is next to a pub/restaurant called The Smithy Pond which looks out over the water. There are plenty of large bream present which are caught on maggot or sweetcorn. A few locals go after the large carp with luncheon meat. Keepnets can be used here but carp over 5lb must be put straight back in. The depth is around 12 feet, opposite the pub. In the summer months weed covers a large area of the lake. An excellent winter pike water, some run to 25lbs.

Types of Fish: Carp, bream, roach, perch, tench and pike.

Rules/Bans: Barbless hooks only.
No carp over 5lb in keepnets.

Number of Lakes: One   **Sat Nav:** S42 6LN

Facilities:

Telephone: 01245 251777 Clay Cross Angling

39

Woodland Farm Fisheries
Ward Lane, Barlborough, Derbyshire.

SAT S43 4JD NAV

Ticket Price: Day tickets £5.00.
OAP's and juniors £4.00.

Direction: From Sheffield head for Junction 30 of the M1.
Just before the junction turn left, sign posted Barlborough
Village. Ward Lane is on the left when you reach the shops.
Follow the lane to the bottom where you will find the fishery.

Description: The fishery has something for everyone, with 82
pegs over four lakes there's plenty for match, pleasure and
specimen anglers. Ice House Lake and Bluebell Lake
contain the larger fish with carp to 26lbs. Island Pond holds
carp to around 7lb with roach, orfe, ide, and skimmers.
Kingfisher Lake has a mixture of silver fish and carp up to
15lb.

Types of Fish: Carp, rudd, roach, bream, ide, orfe.

Rules/Bans: Keepnets only in matches.
No night fishing. Barbless hooks only

Number of Lakes: Four

Sat Nav: S43 4JD
to the top of the lane.

Facilities:

Telephone: 0114 2653541 or 07771 851185

40

Derbyshire Rivers

Whilst the rivers in Derbyshire are not classified as chalk streams, they do run through a band of limestone which provides the rivers with the gin-clear clarity of chalk streams. The limestone strata also gives the rivers a high pH which in turn enriches with nutrients leading to an abundance of river flora and fauna.

River Derwent

The Derwent, at some 50 or so miles in length, is the longest river in Derbyshire. Apart from it's short passage through the City of Derby, it is a completely rural river, finally joining the River Trent just south of Derby. The Derwent's source is at Swain's Greave on Howden Moor on the flank of Bleaklow Hill.

The upper reaches offer some good fly fishing with plenty of trout and grayling, and beyond Matlock an increasing number of coarse fish are found including barbel and chub.

River Dove

The River Dove rises on the slopes of Axe Edge, close to the Leek to Buxton road and runs southwards for 45 miles to join the River Trent forming for much of its course, the south-west border between Derbyshire and Staffordshire. Although only a stream, the river Dove has a pronounced valley within half a mile of it's source. Beresford Dale is associated with Izzak Walton and his friend, though 40 years his junior, Charles Cotton, and the 17th century classic 'The Compleat Angler or The Contemplative Man's Recreation'. The River Dove is no doubt one of the most picturesque and important fly fishing rivers in the world. The river enjoys healthy hatches throughout the year and no one should miss the mayfly fishing when the fish enjoy a veritable feast for two weeks or so. The mayfly hatches on the river Dove are as spectacular as those found on the Test and Itchen.

River Lathkill

The River Lathkill must be one of Derbyshire's smallest rivers, but its interest and beauty easily make it one of the most impressive and it is a very popular tourist destination in the Peak District National Park. Much of the valley is part of the Derbyshire Dales National Nature Reserve and includes a Scheduled Ancient Monument, designated for its lead mine remains. The upper reach of the river is a Site of Special Scientific Interest (SSSI) and a candidate Special Area of Conservation under the European Union Habitats Directive.

The River Lathkill and its dale can be accessed from several points along its length, but it is from the ancient lead mining village of Monyash across a hilly pasture that the top of the Lathkill ravine is reached. A narrow gap between towering walls of limestone where the floor is littered with rocks shattered by winter frosts, leads down into a narrow gully. The way opens out a little and opposite is a low cave under the cliff from which the old watercourse emerges, although in drier times the first springs are lower down.

The bed of the stream is thick with weed down to where Cales Dale comes in from the right. Here the trees begin and the right hand side slopes of the valley are densely wooded, while on the opposite side the white rock is weathered into strange shapes. Soon the course clears and the river flows briskly over a stony bed. The Lathkill now stretches ahead, a fine sheet of water with limestone cliffs on either side. If the deserted upper stretches are wild and abandoned, the lower reaches are friendly and full of tranquil beauty, the haunt of dippers and water voles.

River Wye

The River Wye rises on Axe Edge above Buxton and flows in a south-easterly direction through Buxton and Bakewell to join the Derwent at Rowsley, 15 miles later.

The Wye is a popular trout fishing river, frequently stocked for syndicates, hotels and others who pay for the fly fishing. The limestone gives the river it's lifeblood, enriching it with nutrients and giving it an alkaline nature. This leads to an abundance of insect life, thriving in the rich weed beds. The Wye trout quickly grow to large proportions on this heady diet of shrimps, sedges, upwing flies and many other invertebrates. The river is most famous for it's naturally breeding population of rainbow trout.

Information kindly supplied by fishpal.com

River Derwent at Matlock Bath

Dale Road, Matlock Bath.

SAT NAV DE4 3NS

Ticket Price: River Derwent at Matlock Bath
Available from Newsagents Matlock Bath (opposite the pavilion car park) Day membership £5.00
Day membership shall at all times be bound by the rules of Matlock Angling Club.

Directions: From Matlock take the A6. The stretch of river is in the centre of Matlock Bath.

Description: The stretch at Matlock Bath has day tickets available, all other stretches are members only. The river has many differing parts, shallow and fast and slow and deep and various fish holding spots along its length. The stretch at Matlock Bath was restocked with 3500 coarse fish from the Environment Agency in 2007, these were roach, barbel and dace from 3-6 inches. Some of the banks to the pegs are steep and caution should be taken when fishing these spots especially when the river is carrying extra water.

Types of Fish: The river contains, grayling to 2lbs, barbel to 6lbs, chub to 4lbs, roach to 2lbs, perch to 2lbs, dace to 4oz, gudgeon to 2oz, brown trout to 3lbs, rainbow trout including some wild fish to 3lbs. A few Carp to 5lbs can be found near the aquarium.

41

Information kindly supplied by Matlock Angling Club.

River Trent at Swarkestone
Swarkestone Bridge.

SAT
DE73 7GT
NAV

Ticket Price: This section of the River Trent is run by the Derbyshire Railway Angling Club. Membership is open to all. There are three categories of Annual Membership:

Coarse Only   45.00
Trout and Coarse 75.00
Junior (under 16) 5.00

Description: At Swarkestone our fishing starts a few hundred yards above the bridge on the Melbourne (south) bank. Access to the section is good with parking on the bank above the Bridge and a locked access track downstream of the Bridge.

Above the bridge the river is deep and slow, the main species being roach, perch, bream, plus a few carp and barbel. If the river is high the pegs just above the bridge are usually fishable.

Below the bridge the river is more varied with shallower, faster gravel runs and riffles, and produces good catches of roach, dace, chub and barbel particularly during the summer months. The section below the Bridge regularly produces double figure barbel.

The swims in the 1st and 2nd fields downstream are 4-6 feet deep with a gravel bottom and are ideal for

either barbel or stick / waggler fishing for silver fish.

42

Information kindly supplied by Derbyshire Railway Angling Club.

Keep a record of all your fishing trips with

Log-it

Venue:		Address:			Date:
Peg No:	Start Time:		End Time:	Weather Conditions:	

Species	Weight	Method	Rig set up	Ground Bait	Hook Bait	Time

Venue:		Address:			Date:
Peg No:	Start Time:		End Time:	Weather Conditions:	

Species	Weight	Method	Rig set up	Ground Bait	Hook Bait	Time

Venue:		Address:			Date:
Peg No:	Start Time:	End Time:	Weather Conditions:		

Species	Weight	Method	Rig set up	Ground Bait	Hook Bait	Time

Tackle 2 *Fish*

Angling Supplies

Unit 27, Penistone Road Trading Estate, Penistone Road, Sheffield, S6 2FL

www.tackle2fish.co.uk

e-mail: sales@tackle2fish.co.uk

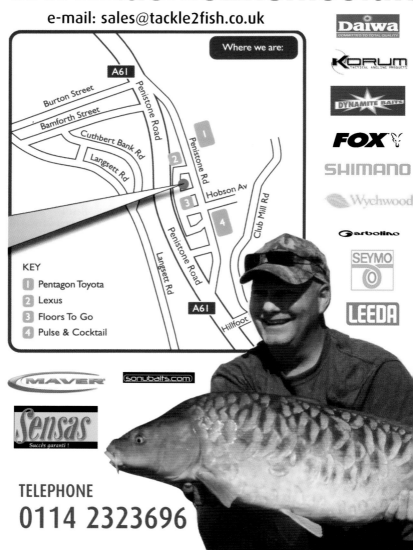

Where we are:

A61

Burton Street

Bamforth Street

Penistone Road

Cuthbert Bank Rd

Langsett Rd

Penistone Rd

1

2

3

Hobson Av

Club Mill Rd

4

Penistone Road

Langsett Rd

A61

Hillfoot

KEY

1 Pentagon Toyota
2 Lexus
3 Floors To Go
4 Pulse & Cocktail

TELEPHONE
0114 2323696

F I S H I N G   T E R M S

Here is a list of the words most commonly used. This will help anglers new to the sport to understand fishing terms used by other anglers.

BALE ARM: A revolving arm on a fixed spool reel which winds line onto the spool.

BAGGING UP: A term used when an angler is catching really well, or to describe a venue that is fishing well.

BAIT BANDS: These are small rubber bands. They are aimed at securing difficult to hook baits to the hook. They come in various sizes to accommodate the size of the bait.

BAITING NEEDLE: These pull the hair loop through the bait. They have a mechanism for attaching to the loop whether it is like a small hook, or a pivot that hooks over the loop. The needle is then drawn back through the bait taking the loop and hair with it.

BARBLESS: A type of hook without sharp barbs to help retain bait and fish. Barbed hooks are banned from most fisheries.

BIN LIDS: A slang term for large bream.

BITE ALARMS: These are electronic sensors that detect the movement of line caused by the fish. They usually have an audible alarm or light to alert the angler.

BIVIES: These are domed tents with an opening at the front providing a shelter from the elements.

BOILIES: These are generally hard balls of bait that are primarily designed as a carp bait.

BREAD PUNCH: A bread punch has a circular 'punch' at the end which is pushed down onto a slice of bread and cuts a small piece out which is placed on the hook. There are many different sizes of punches for different hook sizes.

BREAKING STRAIN: The amount of pressure a line will take before snapping.

BUMPED OFF: This term is used by pole anglers, whereby through the use of heavy tactics the fish once hooked is bumped off. This happens when the fish is not big enough to expand the elastic fully.

CASTERS: The chrysalis form of a maggot.

DEADBAITING: The use of dead fish for catching predatory fish such pike, perch, and eels.

DISGORGER: A long device to help remove the hook from a fish's mouth. Always have one with you.

FOUL HOOKED: A fish that has been hooked anywhere else on the body apart from the mouth.

GROUNDBAIT: A dry mixture intended to be thrown into the water to attract fish. Usually consists of bread crumb, crushed biscuit, crushed hemp or other ingredients.

HAIR RIG: A hair rig is generally a piece of line that extends beyond the point of the shank of the hook. On the end of the length of line is a small loop.

HOOKLENGTH: A short length of line, of lesser breaking strength than the mainline, to which the hook is tied. It is used to make it less likely to be detected by the fish. It also ensures that if the line is snapped by a fish, the angler would not then lose the float / swim feeder / leger and all the other shot

LEGERING: Bait held on the bottom by means of a weight or feeder.

LOOSEFEED: Small offerings of loose bait, such as maggots or sweetcorn, which are thrown into the water to keep the fish interested in the area you are fishing.

LINE BITES: False indications of bites usually caused by fish brushing against the line.

LURES: Artificial fish, used to tempt predators such as pike and zander.

MARGIN: This is an area nearest the bank, that has a shallower depth than that of the main water.

MATCH FISHING: A competitive form of coarse fishing which involves people drawing out a random peg (a place to fish), and then trying to catch as many fish as possible within the allotted time. Usually the winner will be the one with the greatest weight of fish caught.

PEG: A peg is a pre defined fishing area. Venues are split up into evenly spaced fishing zones which are often marked with a wooden peg or marker.

PINKIES: The larvae of the green bottle fly. Small, very lively and great as a loosefeed on stillwaters and canals or as a hookbait for smaller fish.

PLUMMET: A device used for determining the depth of the water in which you are fishing.

POLE: A pole is constructed from very advanced carbon combinations and comes in various sizes, weight and prices.

POLE RIG: These are lengths of line that have the float, weights and a hook attached.

QUIVER TIP: A special type of rod used to detect bites when ledgering. It has a sensitive tip that curves over when the angler has a bite. Quiver tips vary in strength and stiffness which can be changed according to the weather conditions.

SNAGS: Features in your swim that are likely to cause you problems They can also be fish holding features such as lilies, overhanging trees, sunken branches. A place to avoid once a fish is hooked.

SPADE END HOOKS: Spade end hooks have an up-turned flattened piece of metal instead of an eye to which to tie the fishing line.

SPECIMEN: A term given to any fish that is a particularly good size for its species.

STRIKE: To respond to the taking of the bait by pulling the rod in an upwards or sideways motion to hook the fish.

SWIM: The area of water where you are fishing.

Tackle: A term used to refer to any fishing equipment (photo tackle)

TEST CURVE: The test curve is the time and weight needed to make the tip bend 90 degrees from the rod butt. Each rod has a test curve with those being used for specimen fish such as carp having a greater test curve than a general coarse rod.

TROTTING: Allowing a float to travel at the speed of the current.

WHIP: This is a scaled down version of a pole.

DERBYSHIRE TACKLE SHOPS

Alfreton Angling Centre, 11 Park St, Alfreton, DE55 7JE.   Tel: 01773 832611

Angling Centre Derby, 27-33 Nightingale Rd, Derby, DE24 8BG.   Tel: 01332 380605

Arundel Angling Supplies, 56 Arundel street, Glossop, SK13 7AB.   Tel: 01457 866727

Bacchus and Rhone, 127-129 High Street, Woodville, DE11 7DU.   Tel: 01283 216870

Burton Angling Supplies, 30 Borough Rd, Burton-on-Trent   Tel: 01283 548540

Chaddesden Angling, Mercaston Road, Chaddesden DE21 4HU   Tel: 01332 671458

Clay Cross Angling, 51 High St, Clay Cross, Chesterfield, S45 9DX.   Tel: 01246 251777

Cliff Madden Angling, 5 Church St, Staveley, Chesterfield, S43 3TL.   Tel: 01246 472410

Climax Fishing Tackle, 2 Stubley Hollow, Dronfield, S18 1PP.   Tel: 01246 412233

Dave's Tackle, 26a Chesterfield Rd, Staveley, Chesterfield, S43 3QF.   Tel: 07879 483418

Derbyshire Fishing Flies, 82 Heathway, Hatton, Derby, DE65 5EP.   Tel: 01283 813734

Derwent Angling Centre, 110 Bridge Street, Belper, DE56 1AZ.   Tel: 01773 828911

Dragon Carp Direct, Unit 3, Calow Brook Drive, Chesterfield, S41 0DR. Tel: 01246 540140

Fishermania, 714-716, Harvey Rd, Derby, DE24 0EG.   Tel: 01332 752500

Fly Fishing Shop, 3a Hebden Court, Matlock St, Bakewell, DE45 1EE. Tel: 01629 813531

Fort Angling, 2 Station Rd, Borrowash, Derby, Derbyshire, DE72 3LG. Tel: 01332 662379

Leegem Angling Centre, 81 Sheffield Rd, Chesterfield, S41 7LT.   Tel: 01246 559480

Max Tackle, 13 Rectory Rd, Clowne, Chesterfield, S43 4BH.   Tel: 01246 812476

Melbourne Tackle & Gun, 64 High St, Melbourne, Derby, DE73 8EJ.   Tel: 01332 862091

Nathan's of Derby, 9-19 Edgeware Rd, Mackworth, Derby, DE22 4EW. Tel: 01332 523630

Redfins Angling, 12a Fenton Crescent, Measham, DE12 7EU   Tel: 01530 272864

Rod & Line Tackle, 17 Nottingham Rd, Ripley, DE5 3DJ.   Tel: 01773 749545

Simpsons Tackle, 17 Old Road, Whaley Bridge, High Peak, SK23 7HS. Tel: 01663 734220

Stephen Woolley, The Woodyard, Belle Vue Rd, Ashbourne, DE6 1AT. Tel: 01335 300095

Tackle Box, 323 Somercotes Hill, Somercotes, Alfreton, DE55 4JX.   Tel: 01773 307458

Taylor's Tackle, 136 Cotmanhay Rd, Ilkeston, DE7 8NZ.   Tel: 0115 9301610

Tibshelf Angling Centre, 5 Newton Rd, Tibshelf, Alfreton, DE55 5PH.   Tel: 01773 872280

Tommo's Tackle, 653 London Rd, Alvaston, Derby, DE24 8UQ.   Tel: 01332 861744

I N D E X

If you know of a fishery that you would like including in one of these fish-it guides or you want to update an existing venue. Please fill in the form below.

Fishery Name

Fishery Address

Post code

Contact Name

Telephone No

Adult Day Ticket Price	£	concession OAP'S	£

Fish species and approximate weights

Brief Description

Rules / Bans

Facilities

Number of Lakes

Please e-mail or post a colour photo for inclusion in the next publication.

Please return this form to:
Arc Publishing
166 Knowle Lane,
Bents Green,
Sheffield S11 9SJ.

chris_keeling@tiscali.co.uk

New Fishery ☐

Update to Fishery ☐

New Fishery / Fishery Update Form

Fish-it

DISCOVER NEW PREVIOUSLY UNPUBLISHED LOCATIONS

These regional fishing guides are packed with a wide range of information on lakes, ponds, canals, reservoirs and rivers. Each venue has a full colour page detailing ticket prices, directions, species of fish, facilities available and contact details. There are photos of each venue as well as useful tips on which peg to fish and best baits to use.

Tel: **07809 172872**